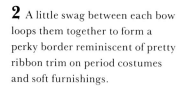

2 A little swag between each bow loops them together to form a perky border reminiscent of pretty ribbon trim on period costumes and soft furnishings.

1 Use a medium artist's brush to stencil the small bow, using a stippling brush action for the neatest results. Precision matters more with small patterns, on surfaces examined close to, like furniture, accessories. Pick up colour a little at a time, testing on rough paper.

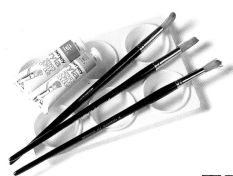

Stencilling is as easy as painting by numbers. Using fast-drying acrylic artists' colours, and either traditional straight-cut stencil brushes, or firm bristled artists' brushes as shown, follow our step-by-step instructions for perfect results.

THE ART OF BOWS

or Easy Steps to Perfect Stencilling

Keep equipment to a minimum to begin with: acrylic colours and bristle brushes available from any art shop, matt white emulsion paint (handy for softening and extending artists' colours), plus masking tape to hold the stencil in place, a plate for mixing colours, and a damp cloth for tidying up any mistakes.

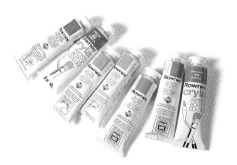

4 Stencil in exactly the same way, but you may find tabs of masking tape helpful to steady the triple row while you stencil. Use the same medium brush, and minimum colour, as always, testing each time on rough paper.

5 The striped swag links two bows together. Try to keep the ends of the swag in line with the inside stripe on the bow (see the picture). This is especially important if you plan to add the bunched ribbon tail to the design, because it needs space to fit under the bow knot.

3 Stencil a 'tail' beneath each bow, and the border gains a whole new dimension. This is a dramatic shape, good for filling bigger spaces.

6 Stencil all the bows and swags first, using a pencilled guide line round a room, for instance, where the ceiling line may dip and wander (almost always in old houses). Having blocked in the border, go back and add the tails, as here.

Showing that you can't have too much of a good thing: our be-ribboned bedroom, its warm buff walls and white wood-work glamourised by our Ribbon stencil set.

TYING THE KNOT: QUIET ROMANCE

There are bows and swags on almost everything in sight, if you look closely, but the effect is not the least bit fussy or frilly. Colour choice is what sets the mood: if you want the feminine look, *use pale blue or pink over antique white (what decorators call 'dirty' white; add raw umber to paint). Note how stopping the wall colour at picture rail level, and emphasising with stencils, makes a tall room seem less lofty.*

Plain chairs like this used to be relegated to the bathroom or playroom, but its functional appearance has been transformed with a few stencils. Note how prettily the ribbon 'tail', doubled, draws attention to the back of the chair, and how cleverly four bows linked by mini swags 'frame' the square seat, substituting for a cushion and tying up with bows and tails on the shutter panels.

Mini bows and ribbons are a classic device for showing up the shape of furniture surfaces in a decorative way. Here a simple oak veneer bedside cupboard, given a 'limed' finish to lighten it, has been brightened with stencilling in the same red as the walls. The bunched tails and bows on the wall behind have been planned to line up with the top.

Mini bows are perfect too for dressing up room accessories effectively and quickly. Anyone at all can stencil four bows on a cheap card lampshade, but what a lot of class they add. It's the handmade touch that can make mass-produced items graciously personal. Take care to stencil crisply and clearly on an item like this: use the minimum of paint and test the brush on rough paper each time.

The final inspiration was to use the striped swag to make a lattice design stencilled on to plain creamy cotton sheeting, to make budget curtains with one-off prestige. On fabric stencil just the same way, but use special fabric paints (Dylon colourfun, Le Franc & Bourgeois) which are machine-washable when the stencilling is sealed by ironing with a warm iron. Cotton cord makes an appropriate tie-back.

HINTS OF RIBBON TO FINISH

It's Attention to Detail that Makes the Difference

Most of the ideas suggested here for using your Ribbon stencils can be painted in a few minutes, but that little extra bit of time and care adds a real 'decorator' touch to a room scheme. Carrying a stencil theme through to fabrics, furniture and accessories is a pretty way of linking everything together visually and, as our pictures show, cheap plain lampshades and painted junk furniture shoot straight upmarket.